The Day the Church Cried

Contents

Foreward; Understanding Africa 1

Attentive; Paying close attention to YAH 9

Faithful; Remaining loyal and steadfast; true to the original 24

Real; Not an imitation or artificial; to be genuine 35

Integrity; Being honest with strong morals, adhering to them even in the dark 46

Compassion; Concern for the sufferings or misfortunes of others .. 57

Authenticity; The quality of being real or true 71

Closing Remarks; The Day the Church Cried 82

Understanding Africa

Attentive **F**aithful **R**eal **I**ntegrity **C**ompassion **A**uthenticity

"For GOD so greatly loved the world that He gave His one and only begotten Son, so that whoever believes and trusts in Him shall not perish, but have eternal life" - ***John 3 v 16***

When I started on this journey to set up a movement called Roots with my friend Steve, we had to dig deep to understand why GOD had called us on this mission…What did the mission mean? Why did it feel so important? Why when putting together the words we believed GOD had placed on our hearts, a rearranging of their initials spelt out "AFRICA"?

It would take over a decade for me to begin answering these questions. As 2020 came along, I realized it was time to head down the Rabbit Hole, to see just how deep it goes…

When the concept of false narratives is brought up, especially within the Christian community, it's surprising how easily this is laughed off. The idea that false narratives would be created by those in charge, the ones who give us our daily consumption of information, seems to elude today's body of believers…

I find this strange when I look at the teaching of our Adonai and Saviour; the very husband of the body of believers known today as the church. Many of His disagreements were aimed towards the Pharisees, Sadducees, Scribes and Teachers of the law. These are the very people who oversaw the narrative and information consumed by those who lived within the Israelite communities.

So, what are the false narratives that I think are key to the season we're in as a people…

- Systemic Racism does not exist
- Faith cannot solve Political and Social issues
- GOD is a globalist first, an individual and nationalist after

Black Lives Matter

The George Floyd murder in 2020 hit me harder than I ever thought a death like that would. There have been many untimely deaths of Black people at the hands of ignorance. It's a regular occurrence, so not something new. However, something about the death of a man, begging for life under the crux of another person's knee, for nearly 10 minutes, cut my soul in a way I had never felt before.

I started on what I thought was a downward spiral, but it ended up being a journey of enlightenment and education, that had evaded me for nearly 40 years. What does it mean to be Black? Why do Black people seem to suffer more across the world? Why are Africans still suffering persecution in America 400 years later, when slavery ended centuries ago? More importantly, what does the Bible have to say on this subject and is the church important in this?

My childhood had an interesting backdrop. Born in the UK to Nigerian parents, the first generation to travel here. I grew up with elderly White foster parents for nearly 18 years, and often found myself struggling to mix 3 cultures – White British, Black British and Black African.

As I manoeuvred through this maze of mental complexities and cultural phenomena, I always queried the pull on many Africans to come to the Western world. To name their children with western middle names. To seek after the western idiom of dress sense, hair acceptance and saviour needs. It seemed illogical to me. Were there no Black voices across the diaspora that pioneered African ingenuity? Was the African concept of female identity and expression so wrong, compared to the westernised feminist movement? Would Africa always need help from the West, as they recovered from the decimating impacts of Colonialism?

As you can see my childhood only ever seemed to raise more questions, than answers. Yet I had my faith in Jesus Christ. The mousey brown haired, occasionally darker haired, saviour, who died for me on a wooden cross; rendering any other thought or desire powerless…or so I assumed!?

I would go through my formative years and into early adulthood with this mantra at my side – understanding culture can be complex, but all is ok because Jesus died for me. It would be many years later as I journeyed through my own heritage, that I'd realise how intertwined the two had always been…never distinct or in opposition to each other.

For all the cultural identity struggles I faced, I was still very blessed by both my natural and foster family. I would be given opportunities in life that many Black kids from inner city Birmingham did not get. I would also be encouraged to stand firm in my identity without being driven by a media narrative, a playground commentary, or a parental desire.

Thus, if I faced any acts of discrimination or inequality, they would usually get buried or passed off as naivety or some form of ignorance that was not worth investing time to resolve. The idea of a system set up to enforce those inequalities, was alien to me. If I really thought about it, I'd dare say it was an idea beyond my worst nightmares!

It was only after the death of George Floyd, that I took some time to unravel the parts of my life that had impacted me more than I realised. The subtle and not so subtle comments. The "no" answers received, that had no merit. The expectation bias that, had it not been for a handful of great teachers in my life, would have inhibited where I've got to today. This journey, painful as it was, was opening my crying eyes to the reality of something big. A lot bigger than I could have imagined. Something so deep, that a simple call for unity and removal of prejudice, would not be enough to ensure everyone could be a winner.

It was now that I started to understand why GOD was calling me back to the Roots of my faith all those years ago, and why AFRICA was key to that!

The Origins of Christianity

I was a strategy analyst for just under 15 years. Much of my work was to design strategies to help change customer behaviour. As I lifted the lid on the systemic racism seemingly pervading every area of life, I needed to put my strategy cap back on. How would you build a strategy that allows you to take control of much of the world, as well as change the thoughts and behaviour of the people?? – Answer – a multi angled approach focused on faith, resource, politics, and race – Each strategy element had been so deeply embedded into the global system, that it had become nigh on impossible to identify the roots of the reality we were living in today. Allow me to explain…

Christianity is one of the most dominant faiths in the world today. It is the one faith that is prevalent in not only most civilisations, but also most political agendas. The faith is accompanied with a mousey brown-haired, blue-eyed saviour, as the pinnacle for it. The most popular worship songs worldwide are written by Western authors. The known format of a modern-day church service is consistent, whether you're in India or Indianapolis.

Yet the faith actually started with a handful of followers who were not White. Worship was sometimes less structured in its offering. The origins of the faith were connected to an older religion, stemming from the Horns of Africa, with a simple message and not one motivated to take over nations politically. And as for the saviour himself?? Well, let's look at some thoughts…

Jesus' parents escaped to Egypt; a land at the time that was not as we see today, but full of people more melanated in their pigment. Why would they do that?

"…*his eyes like flaming torches, his arms and legs like the gleam of burnished bronze*…" *- Daniel 10 v 6*

"…*one like a son of man… The hairs of his head were White, like White wool, like snow. His eyes were like a flame of fire, his feet were like burnished bronze*…" *- Revelation 1 v 13-15*

– try googling burnished bronze

The race of Christ is a whole book in itself, so not something I intend to spend time on here. However, based off those simple passages of scripture, you would be right to believe that the saviour, and indeed his people the Israelites, were what we would class today as Black people. What's more, we see in many of the history books written by western conquerors who came across the Israelites, that they were described as Negroes with woolly hair. To top it all off, scientific evidence also shows us that life in all its fullness began in Africa. It is believed that every human being alive today can trace their ancestry to there. And some of the earliest civilisations originate from there.

So how does a faith that originated in Africa, manage to take over the world spiritually and politically under the guise of a White saviour? How do we see a completely different perception of the original people and original saviour?

Answer – witchcraft and smart narratives, mainly through the power of media. Two things that are essentially one and the same – Media and Medium!

The embedding of systemic racism started with the takeover of a faith, by changing the racial backdrop and context to it. It was then followed by the takeover of the people and the resource. Which then gave the relevant power needed to take over the politics…and voila…here we are! A wide-reaching strategy, that comes straight out of the pits of hell!

Addressing Systemic Racism

Let's imagine you give me the benefit of the doubt and assume that what I'm telling you is right…now what? How do you fix it, if indeed it is worth fixing??

At this point it's easy for some people to jump to the concept of equality, or more recently equity…but what does equity really mean? And is it GOD's will??

Well, let's start with an understanding of what equity is;

"Equity, in its simplest terms as it relates to racial and social justice, means meeting communities where they are and allocating resources and opportunities as needed to create equal outcomes for all community members." - Government Finance Officers Association

Ok, so we're either fixing the system, or putting tools in place to give those who need it, what's required to thrive where they're at. That seems good and fair and something GOD would want, given He tells us to practice justice, love mercy, and walk humbly with Him.

Yet the pitfall comes when we take a broad-brush approach to fix issues, using the same systemic approach that created those issues in the first place. We end up with a new, yet equally bad system of control, which at its worst uses the bible to establish its goal. On the surface it seems great, but a deeper look at end time prophecy highlights this as the exact method the Antichrist will use to try and deceive us all.

I don't intend to explore the topic of the Antichrist and/or the Beast System that the book of Revelation tells us will control much of the world in the end times. However, I do seek to emphasise the dangers of striving for a better world, without going back to the blueprint of that very same world. This is detailed clearly beginning with Genesis, ending with Revelation, served with a side helping of the Book of Enoch, Jubilees, Maccabees, and other Apocrypha and Historical books.

So, let's quickly do that now…

What does the Bible not tell us to do?

Paul's letter to the Galatians gives what many call an insight into equality and its worth;

"There is neither Jew nor Greek, slave nor free, male nor female, for you are all one in Christ Jesus"

- Galatians 3 v 28

This is a verse often used in discussions around gender equality and racism. However, the context behind this passage goes much deeper; it refers to salvation. No longer does your nationality, race, gender, social status, or anything else define whether you can be saved or not. Only through the saving blood and grace of Jesus Christ. Simple.

The bible does not tell us to treat everyone the same, or to not see colour, or not recognise differences and the unique qualities everyone brings to the table.

What does the Bible tell us to do?

The key is to look at what the attributes of the Kingdom of Heaven are. Luke 15 gives us a real insight into the mind of GOD and what a community of GOD should look like. Throughout the passage, it speaks about a place where each individual matters, to the point where you'd leave the whole community to bring back one lost individual. And when you bring them back, it's party time!!!

The bible does tell us to treat everyone as an individual, "because we are fearfully and wonderfully made." Each with their own individual imprint; a DNA designed by the Supreme Creator. And from there, the outputs of equity…justice, love, mercy, and humility…should play out automatically.

All of this sounds easy right; so why are we not there yet? Why has the church not led the way in restoring the broken community and indeed broken world we see around us today? - I seek permission to lay a strong answer at the door of the church; and that is repentance!

Repentance for the churches part in one of the world's worst acts against humanity. An act done to a people who we discussed earlier, were indeed the very same nation that the Messiah came from. Repentance for the churches part in helping to establish a strategy straight from the pits of hell, in the form of Systemic Racism, spearheaded by White Supremacy. Repentance by the church to "turn back" to the blueprint of our faith, to understand just exactly how this world should be working. Not simply following the media or political narrative, which we saw play out so strongly in 2020 and 2021.

Global agendas that we hear so often about making the world a better place? Well, GOD is an individualist first, a nationalist second, and a globalist last. Let that marinate as you read the rest of this book…

Repentance is not just saying sorry. True repentance should see restoration and change; without that, I don't believe we can be truly sorry?!

Let me finish this section with this; If true repentance is all that is needed, then why hasn't the church done this? My answer; It is too far embedded into the system, to truly be the light that the very same system needs!

Faith can, and should change societal and political issues. However, it can only do that through the Word of GOD. If we're only focused on 40% of that Word, then we can never truly bring Kingdom principles to a broken world. We can never bring about true change from the One who does not change. That's why it's time church. Time to come out of the beast system. Time to go back to the Roots of our faith, leaving no stone hidden or any topic off limits. Time to cling to our Saviour like never before. For we are in the last hour…

Please Note that from now on, I will attempt to go back to the Hebraic Roots for the concept of GOD and Jesus. I feel led by the Holy Spirit to use the ancient Hebrew dialect of YHWH and Yeshua (sometimes called Yahushua Hamashiach), as opposed to GOD and Jesus Christ. I will also aim to capture the oneness nature of the Father and Son interaction; in those situations I will use the term YAH.

ATTENTIVE
– Paying close attention to YAH

" ...for there is nothing concealed that will not be disclosed, or hidden that will not be made known. What I tell you in the dark, speak in the daylight; what is whispered in your ear, proclaim from the roofs." -
Matthew 10 v 26 - 27

There's something quite selfless in the art of being attentive. It goes deeper than just listening occasionally to something or someone, but speaks to a desire to attend to the need of another.

In a marriage, being attentive is a key feature to aid a long marriage. Understanding the need of another and meeting that need is a strong foundation for any relationship. And it's this very concept that YHWH calls us to as believers and followers of his son Yeshua.

The image of Yeshua coming to meet his bride, aka the body of believers; is an image etched very much in the mind of many Christians today. In the meantime, the intimate relationship where the bridegroom whispers to his bride all types of truth and revelations, has powerful implications for now. It gives us a clear guide on how we ought to conduct ourselves, as we wait for that moment.

Knowledge of YAH

What should waiting for that moment mean for us and our daily walk with YAH?

How important is He to us and how important are His words to us; both past and present?

The story of the misguided prophet's servant, gives a clear picture of someone who is in tune with their Elohim, as opposed to someone who is not. Someone who recognises how important YHWH is to them, compared to someone who is oblivious to the army of Heaven stood around them.

"Do not be afraid, for those who are with us are more than those who are with them."

– 2 Kings 6 v 16

What makes the difference so clear and obvious? Knowledge of who you are dealing with!

A large number of Christians today have what they'd describe as a strong faith. They attend church every Sunday. Pray every morning and evening. Show love to their fellow person. Volunteer in the church's missionary projects. Whilst this initially sounds amazing, the gap comes for many with the depth of their knowledge. When challenged on aspects of their faith, many struggle to articulate the reason for the hope that they have. Also, when faced with times of fear and trembling, many struggle to rely on the firm foundation of their faith.

Knowledge of YAH comes through a real understanding of who He said He is, what He has done, what He says He will do, and everything that Yeshua is. All of that can be found in the scriptures; the 66-book canon in itself is sufficient, but other scriptures like the book of Enoch, add to the depth of the knowledge one should have in their faith.

Yet the church still finds most of its Sunday sermons revolve around the New Testament teachings of Yeshua and Paul. Again, whilst this seems to make perfect sense, you can never fully understand someone until you understand the backdrop of who they are. Paul and Yeshua were from the Tribes of Israel (Benjamin and Judah respectively) and their characteristics, traditions, attributes, and history tied back to those Israelite roots. So, when Paul is talking about circumcision and debating its need for new believers, a genuine understanding into the act and relevance of circumcision is fundamental. This is also the case when the curtain of the temple is torn in two when the Messiah dies. Understanding the significance of the curtain, the temple, and the punishment for those in the Old Testament times who didn't appropriately acknowledge that significance, is key!

Unfortunately, very little time is spent in the whole bible, especially addressing difficult passages; like why did Satan approach YHWH's throne, when the angels were presenting themselves? Or what exactly were those Angel/Human hybrids doing in the days of Noah, to pollute the earth so thoroughly that YHWH would destroy it? This depth of knowledge is sometimes lacking in the church and this reality was laid bare in 2020, as a global terror ran rife throughout the church. It generated fear and caused many believers to cry out like Elisha's servant, **"Oh no, my master! What are we to do?"** – 2 Kings; 6 v 15

Across three different people in the Bible, several significant statements around the concept of love are given, which make up the blueprint to life;

1. **1 John 4 v 18** "There is no fear in love. But perfect love drives out fear"
2. **Matthew 22 v 37** "Love YAH your Elohim with all your heart and with all your soul and with all your mind"
3. **John 14 v 15** "If you love me, keep my commands"
4. **Ecclesiastes 12 v13** "Fear YAH and keep His commandments; for this is the whole duty of man"

The overarching theme to these statements is the concept of love in the *doing* sense. Having a reverential fear for YAH and *doing* what He says. This way there can be no fear generated from elsewhere, because you are walking in the light of the word; a lamp before your feet. And whilst it sounds simple, this doing act can only come from a place of greater understanding into YAH.

From the ten commandments, to the 600+ laws of life. From the words of the prophets, to the words of YAH's messengers. From the acts of judgement, to the words of YAH's people. Each and every fingerprint, a mark of YAH that helps you gain better understanding into the foundation that is His very Word; the Rock to build your foundation on.

I hope by now it has become clear how important it is to read the Word of YAH. Not only to read it, but to gain understanding and insight from it too. This is the first and best way to understand our part in the marriage to the Messiah. To be attentive to what is needed from us in this new covenant (contract) signed with blood. Whilst you master this, there are other attributes that can aid an attentive mindset that is always seeking the will of YAH through Yeshua. And it is through the acts of Yeshua that we see many of these attributes play out.

Silence

He was the master at it! Whether it was in a moment of crisis where an angry mob are baying for the blood of an adulterous woman. Or whether it's before a highly feared judge who believed he held the power of life and death over the Messiah. The art of silence was often used by Yeshua, and was a great way to show the power of words. When he spoke out of those moments of silence, what was said carried such weight and are indeed words that still resonate with us today.

"Let him who is without sin cast the first stone"

- John 8 v 7

There were also times when Yeshua opted for solitude and in those moments sought to be alone in silence. Sometimes through grief, sometimes just to reconnect to the Father. All in all, it's a lesson for us, especially in a world where everyone has an opinion on everything, and feels the need to comment on anything. It teaches us that we should be silent more and use those moments to see what we can learn, hear and notice.

Patience

Imagine you were the Word of YAH. Imagine that for you and by you all things were made. Imagine if you were the first and the last; Alpha and Omega. Now imagine you came to earth, only to be lied to, spat on, beaten, betrayed and lynched. Imagine you had to explain and re-explain fundamentals to people, who you expected to know and understand them already. What would you need in abundance to deal with this?

Patience, Patience, and more Patience!

Alongside the levels of patience that Yeshua had to show in dealing with the above scenarios, some of the greatest acts of patience were displayed towards individuals. His patience with hot headed Peter, who often missed the point in the Messiah's whole ministry. His patience with James and John (and their mum), who felt it ok to ask for greatness in heaven. His patience with doubting Thomas, who should have known and believed that his Elohim was coming back to life. His patience with Saul (aka Paul), who was actively persecuting His followers.

There are many other acts and signs of patience from the Messiah, displayed in parables, or as emphasised by the Apostle Peter who exclaimed;

"YAH is not slow in keeping his promise, as some understand slowness. Instead, he is <u>patient</u> with you, not wanting anyone to perish, but everyone to come to repentance."

– 2 Peter 3 v 9

So why is patience important? Because it gives chance for reflection, revelation, and restoration

The 3 R's

Reflection is a word used almost as little as the act itself in today's society. In a fast-paced world demanding immediate gratification, taking the time to stop is a long lost art! In these latter days the church needs to find this art once more.

What does it mean to reflect and what does the bible say about reflection? Reflection speaks into the concept of serious thought and consideration, and this is really brought to life in the letter Paul writes to the Philippian church. By what we know as the fourth chapter of the letter, Paul changes lane from an action focused letter to a thought focused letter in verse 6. He focuses on anxiety and meditation. A call to not be anxious and to trust YAH. A call to meditate on things that are, "noble … just … pure … lovely … good … virtuous … praiseworthy".

This is the act of reflection the apostle Paul is calling us to. Taking serious consideration into what we place our time and thoughts on, ensuring we get the restorative outcome a good reflection period should give.

And that is revelation through Yeshua Hamashiach; the Messiah!

- Revelation of new things we may have seen or heard before, but not paid close attention to. [1]
- Or revelation of the many blessings we are to be thankful for, "…for this is the will of YHWH in Yeshua Hamashiach for you." [2]

In the silent, patient and 360° reflective acts mirroring our Master and Saviour, the attentive mindset is brought closer to YAH. This places us in a good space to try and fulfil our part of the covenant marriage; which takes us onto the final part of our attentive journey. Here we switch our focus slightly away from the actions of The Messiah, and very much onto us and our actions as individuals…

Reap what you Sow

Many people within the church understand The Word of YAH to act like algorithms operating across the universe as we know it. Universal laws that work in perfect harmony to ensure that YAH's Word comes to pass. Outside of the church, this is often mistaken as "karma", but the true sense of the concept for Christians is that you Reap what you Sow. It features in Galatians Chapter 6, verse 7, but there are many other places throughout scripture that this concept is made clear…

- **Job 4 v 8** "As I have seen, those who plow iniquity and sow trouble reap the same."
- **Psalm 126 v 5** "Those who sow in tears shall reap with shouts of joy!"
- **Proverbs 11 v 18** "The wicked earns deceptive wages, but one who sows righteousness gets a sure reward."
- **Jeremiah 17 v 10** "I the Lord search the heart and test the mind, to give every man according to his ways, according to the fruit of his deeds."
- **Hosea 10 v 12** "Sow for yourselves righteousness; reap steadfast love; break up your fallow ground, for it is the time to seek the Lord, that he may come and rain righteousness upon you."
- **Luke 6 v 38** "Give, and it will be given to you. Good measure, pressed down, shaken together, running over, will be put into your lap. For with the measure you use it will be measured back to you."
- **2 Corinthians 9 v 6** "The point is this: whoever sows sparingly will also reap sparingly, and whoever sows bountifully will also reap bountifully."

And it is with confidence in this particular algorithm, that we, as individuals, should operate our own level of attentiveness. Not only to prevent a future we don't desire, but to prevent one that is not in line with the will of YAH.

In the Olivet Discourse, which is found in Matthew 24, Yeshua is speaking to his disciples on the Mount of Olives. He is talking about the signs of the impending destruction of Jerusalem and the end of this current age. Now whilst we could spend much time discussing the 50 verses in the chapter, the key verse I want to pull the thread on is verse 32;

"Now learn this lesson from the fig tree: As soon as its twigs get tender and its leaves come out, you know that summer is near."

– Matthew 24 v 32

Here we are given an indication of how it is possible to see the fruit we will reap in our own lives, by the sowing that is blossoming now. It is said that prevention is better than cure, and this is how we can ensure our life is not leading to a harvest of bad fruit, but instead one of good fruit.

And what is that good fruit and how do we know that what we're sowing now is carrying that good fruit? Well it's the Fruit of the Spirit, laid out in Galatians chapter 5; Love, Joy, Peace, Patience, Kindness, Goodness, Faithfulness, Gentleness and Self-Control.

If all of this fruit (*notice the singular aspect here*) is not on display, then now is the time to make that right…in the good times and the bad times.

Now we know what we're sowing, we can start unpicking previous journeys and current ones we are on. This act of attentiveness (paying close attention to the past, present and future), transcends believers into a realm where they can begin unlocking YAH's call on them, truly identifying their purpose.

The concept of purpose is a popular theme in the modern-day church.

- What has YAH called me to do on this earth?
- What is my purpose on this earth?
- Who am I destined to be?

However, without clear understanding of where and who you are currently in YAH, you cannot truly fathom your purpose. So, let's look at some of the actions we need to consider, to be purposeful followers of The Way.

Exceeding Expectation

There were a number of scenarios in the time of Yeshua, where He challenged us to exceed expectations. When the 72 return with joy because they'd seen miracles, Yeshua raised their expectations higher. When He spoke about bringing us life, He added the extra expectation of, "having life to the full". He sees your 5th gear, and raises it to 6th gear every time…so why should we settle for less?! Answer; we shouldn't!

The problem however is that our expectations are not always in the right place. In the book of Luke Chapter 8[3], we see the deliverance of three people. There is the man possessed by a legion of Demons, who were actually terrified of Yeshua as He approached them. No one was ever able to deal with the man and indeed his demonic possession, so expectations would have been low at this point. Then there was the woman who had been bleeding for twelve years. She had seen many healers, but to no avail. And finally, there was Jairus' daughter. Why did Jairus a ruler of the Synagogue, come to Yeshua and literally fall at his feet begging for him to come and heal his daughter? Especially given that many involved with the synagogue during Yeshua's time, held a negative view of Him?

The scriptures don't go into the details of *why* Jairus sought out Yeshua, or *why* the poorly woman pushed through the crowd to touch Yeshua's cloak, or *why* the demon possessed man ran up to the Messiah. However, the thread between these stories showed that each person felt the need to go to the one who exceeds expectations. The one who challenges breakthrough and brings it to fruition.

Now many will say, "Yeshua was YAH himself, so of course He could deliver the breakthrough". However, we read the following in John's gospel…

"Very truly I tell you, whoever believes in me will do the works I have been doing, <u>and they will do even greater</u> things than these, because I am going to the Father."

- John 14 v 12

There you have it! Challenge your expectations to see if they're in the right place...or to readjust if they're in the wrong place, no matter how dark that place may feel.

You cannot fathom and run the purposeful race set before you, without understanding every area and depth to your journey; past, present, and future. Step into your attentive state and align your expectations with YAH. If this means you need to take a fresh look at the same old stories that define your life, looking at them more through the eyes of YAH, then so be it...now is the time!

No Man is an Island

A step back to the time of Adam, shows that working alone was not YHWH's desired approach;

"It is not good for the man to be alone. I will make a helper suitable for him."

- Genesis 2 v 18

Whilst there are verses within scripture that allude to a solitary lifestyle, when it comes to doing the work of YAH, teamwork makes the dreamwork!

A passage often cited in conversations around teamwork and leadership, is the story of Jethro, Moses' father-in-law. Jethro was a Midianite priest who didn't really know YHWH the Elohim Moses served. However, he was aware of the acts in Egypt and the mighty works YHWH was doing for Moses and the Israelites during his time. So, he came with Moses' wife and children to meet Moses on his journeys.

To cut a long story short Jethro proceeded to give advice to Moses on how best to lead the people of YHWH, without Moses confirming that this was the desire of YHWH. This lack of confirmation was surprising, given that Jethro was a priest of the Midianites who were behest to foreign gods. Our clearest indication that this may not have been the way forward, is seen in two resulting actions;

1. The Israelites rebel and start worshipping an idol in the form of a Golden Calf
2. YHWH installs a new leadership system mirroring the heavenly realms and not Jethro's suggestion

In Numbers chapter 11, we hear YHWH say, "Gather to Me seventy men of the elders of Israel, whom you know to be the elders of the people and officers over them…" [4]

This blueprint became the ongoing leadership system that the wandering Israelites would operate with. We see something very similar in the book of Luke...

"After these things the Lord appointed seventy others also, and sent them two by two before His face into every city and place where He Himself was about to go"

- Luke 10 v 1

The bible tells us that we should establish a matter by the mouth of two witnesses. Therefore if we wanted another reference, we could look to the book of Jasher. It is a book that some struggle with as it isn't canon, but let your heart inquire of The Holy Spirit on where you sit with it...

"And God said to the seventy angels who stood foremost before him, to those who were near to him, saying, Come let us descend and confuse their tongues, that one man shall not understand the language of his neighbour, and they did so unto them."

- Jasher 9 v 32 (From the destruction of the Tower of Babel)

It's clear that YAH has a modus operandi, which he established on the earth in different ways. Yet what is key here, is the concept of an attentive mind that seeks to understand the will of the Father and operate in that will, not what we may think is right. Yeshua showed us this in all of His ways.

Although some of us may not easily find 70 friends, we can find people to place around us who we can trust, and learn to trust more as we grow in that trust. Look to your left. Look to your right. Identify the people of worth around you. Not what the world sees as worth, but those with a Godly given beauty. Those who are often unsung heroes. Find them and connect, because no man is meant to be an island!

To conclude on the action of connecting with others to be more purposeful followers of The Way, I'll introduce you to the **Four Point Theory**;

- The four people below are connected, but not to every person;
  - A knows B
  - B knows D
  - D knows C
  - C knows A
  - However, A does not know D and B does not know C

- On many occasions our connections look just like this; based on upbringing, location, mindset, etc…
- However, there are many opportunities out there when we start to explore other connections…

The four-point theory challenges us to step outside our assumptions or immediate connections, to create other connections like the diagram below;

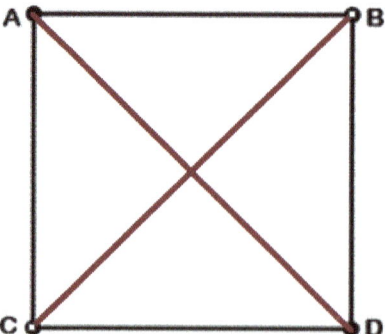

Now everybody knows everyone, and I'm sure the world will become a better place for it!

Final Exhortation on Attentive

Throughout this chapter, we have explored in depth the concept of being attentive. We've looked at different ways to step into this realm of attentiveness; from taking time to reflect, reading the Word, and operating in the Fruit of the Spirit. We've also looked at actions that help us align more with the will of The Most High in this space.

These are just some ways to help bring you closer to the Elohim in who we love, trust and obey. Yet it comes with a warning. A more attentive mindset can take you up a gear and cause you to operate more in the Spiritual realm. As you do this, you may become more open to Spiritual attack. The level of darkness hovering over the earth currently, is straight out of Isaiah chapter 60! The witchcraft, in the form of a Medium that is the Media, has never been as active, or more importantly as effective as it is today.

Without a shadow of a doubt, we are in the times referred to by Paul in his letter to the Thessalonians. The time where people are given over to strong delusion because they do not want to hear the uncomfortable truths. [5]

So, in this season where we need to be at our most attentive and in tune with YAH, we also need to be at our most careful. We will spend some more time on this as we explore spiritual discipline in the faithful arm of this journey. However, for now let me finish with the blessed words of the scriptures…

"Therefore put on the full armour of God, so that when the day of evil comes, you may be able to stand your ground, and after you have done everything, to stand. Stand firm then, with the belt of truth buckled around your waist, with the breastplate of righteousness in place, and with your feet fitted with the readiness that comes from the gospel of peace. In addition to all this, take up the shield of faith, with which you can extinguish all the flaming arrows of the evil one. Take the helmet of salvation and the sword of the Spirit, which is the word of God."

- Ephesians 6 v 13-17

FAITHFUL
– Remaining loyal and steadfast; true to the original

"Then Yeshua said to his disciples, 'Whoever wants to be my disciple must deny themselves and take up their cross and follow me.'" - **Matthew 16 v 24**

Loyalty…another lost art in the modern era?

I don't want to sound like a record on repeat, constantly complaining about the modern age and how much has been lost. So let me ask you a few questions...

1. Do you feel like the average footballer spends less time at a team then they used to? What about managers who haven't been sacked?
2. What do you think the average job tenure is for someone today aged between 20 and 30, compared to before the year 2,000?
3. What do you think the average length of a marriage is in 2022, compared to 1922?

Whilst these queries don't cover all aspects of life, I wonder if like me they make you question whether the concept of loyalty comes as naturally to people as it used to. Maybe it's the instantaneous nature of life today that drives a lack of patience?! Maybe it's the new norm that will never return to the "good old days"?! Either way this reality seems to exist...

So where has the concept of loyalty and remaining faithful fallen down and how do we, especially as the body of believers, set about reaffirming those foundations?!?

My church regularly talks about the aspect of spiritual disciplines. For someone who is very measured and sometimes rigid in his approach to life, disciplines that I can adhere to are like a gift from Heaven.

Before my wife and I married, we went on a marriage preparation course with our pastor and his wife. The course helped us to explore aspects of our marriage that are sometimes taken for granted before entering into the agreement...from bank accounts, to raising children, to who drives the family car, and everything else in between. We found the course to be a light bulb moment in understanding the concept of foundations. Building strong disciplines, that allow you to grow and explore, knowing that your foundations are firm, and your base is intact.

This is what the church was built on and should be standing on today. Disciplines and foundations that are firm and allow a believer to go through the storm and waves, knowing their faith will stand and not be washed away to sea.

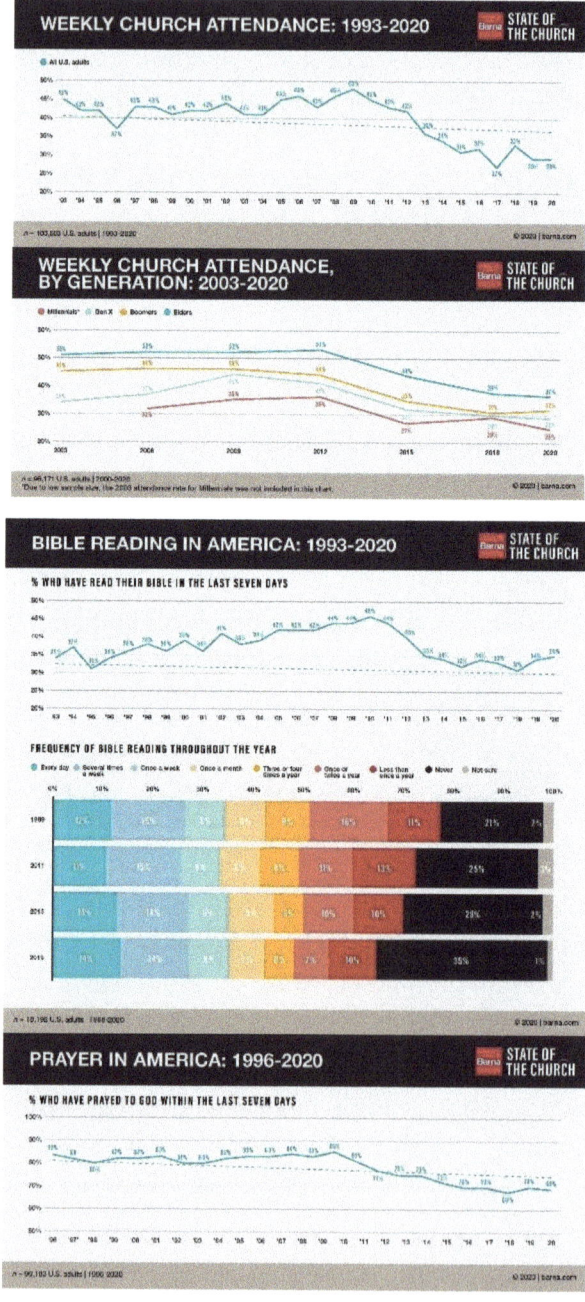

https://www.barna.com/research/changing-state-of-the-church/

Although these figures above are US centric, they show a stark decline over the last decade in what the early church fathers would deem standard disciplines. Things which early believers who were new to the faith, would completely consume and follow without question.

However, as the race to become more "culturally relevant" as Christians has heated up, we've lost the art of building firm foundations. And now we find many Christians falling away from the faith, because of the storms and waves of life, alongside media witchcraft. They find themselves questioning the validity of what YAH said in His Word and through His Word; that is Yeshua Hamashiach.

As a couple, there are some fundamentals my wife and I engage with to help our 10-year marriage continue its growth. We don't always get these right and indeed regularly get it wrong. But we get back in the saddle and hope for the best…

Set Aside Days;

Date Nights for us is as religious as our relationship has been since we got married. With 3 kids and a puppy driving the majority of our focus, setting aside time for just us was key. And that is exactly what the 4th Commandment written by YHWH himself asks us to do;

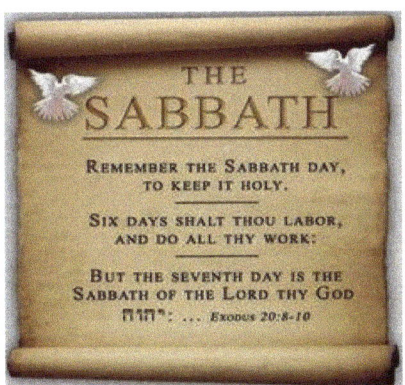

Time set aside for you and YAH…

https://discover.hubpages.com/religion-philosophy/Bible-study-on-the-Sabbath

It's impossible to spend quality time with someone, when the busyness of life uses every spare moment to grab your attention. Ecclesiastes 3 tells us that there is a time for everything. YAH who sees the beginning from the end, knew how important it was to set aside time amidst our daily schedules. Take time to step into a special, sacred moment.

So, what does YAH ask of us? To invest quality time in things of worth, just like you would with your marriage. Recognise your Sabbath and step into communion with Him. And you can start small with little things like Bible reading as a family, gathering with other Christians, spending time with friends sharpening iron. Over time that can build into something more precious and dare I say intimate. To be clear I'm not referring to the false images of intimacy the world has embedded into our minds today.

To get an example of that intimacy, read John 14[6], where Yeshua spends some QT with His disciples before His time on earth comes to an end.

Set Aside Plans;

As a planner and someone who likes to strategise (did I mention that??), I've had to go on a long journey of education into the world of failed plans! Having young kids and just operating in life generally, makes it impossible not to come across best laid plans that fail. And I don't underestimate the concept of a "long journey", because I still struggle with that today; 10 years into marriage.

Yet learning to respond to failed plans, gives you a firm foundation to stand on, so you can deal with all the change that will continue to happen around you.

When Yeshua is delivering the Sermon on the Mount, he spends a little period of time talking about worry. Do not worry about clothes; do not worry about food; do not worry about tomorrow…why? Because YAH has got you. So, when the best laid plans do change, or even when life gets dark, remember who is in control. Store your treasures, your trust and your time with Him.

Be more Peter, less Thomas - *John 20 v 24-29*

Set Aside Trust; Sounds simple right? This concept of trust! But how do you really build it?? Well let's lead by example and go to the Holy Scriptures for guidance…

Then Jesus said to his disciples: "Therefore I tell you, do not worry about your life, what you will eat; or about your body, what you will wear. For life is more than food, and the body more than clothes. Consider the ravens: They do not sow or reap, they have no storeroom or barn; yet God feeds them. And how much more valuable you are than birds! Who of you by worrying can add a single hour to your life? Since you cannot do this very little thing, why do you worry about the rest?

"Consider how the wild flowers grow. They do not labour or spin. Yet I tell you, not even Solomon in all his splendour was dressed like one of these. If that is how God clothes the grass of the field, which is here today, and tomorrow is thrown into the fire, how much more will he clothe you—you of little faith! And do not set your heart on what you will eat or drink; do not worry about it. For the pagan world runs after all such things, and your

Father knows that you need them. But seek his kingdom, and these things will be given to you as well. – Luke 12 v 22-31

A deeper dive of this passage from Luke, highlights some fundamental life choices that Yeshua is asking us to throw aside in an act of prioritisation.

If we didn't truly think about food, clothes, drink and plans for the next day, some of us could become homeless! The bills are constant…the tummies are rumbling…the cold is biting…and that's just for you. What about your spouse; your children; your wider family?? The needs grow and remain at the forefront of our mind. And as the economic world tries to recover from 2 years of carnage, these realities easily move from just a thought, into a genuine worry.

But there is something that Yeshua is asking us to do that is less emotive, and more intentional. It is the intentional act of us making a choice… Am I going to operate in worry and even worse fear, or am I going to set aside an ounce of trust in Him who is called YHWH YIREH; our provider?!

This is emphasised further by Yeshua's brother James (aka Jacob), who explains in detail how our faith cannot stand alone on words, but must be littered with intentional acts; both physically and mentally. These acts can include feeding someone who is hungry or providing clothing to someone who has none. It can also capture the more difficult acts like listening to YAH when everyone else around you thinks something different, or even sacrificing something special to you! Acts that bring to life that true faith, allowing you to move from a trust that seems built on blind faith, to one that is more intentional. [7]

Set Aside Gratitude; The conversation between Yeshua and the Samaritan woman in John Chapter 4, has so many layers to it. Cultural bias…gender bias…religious bias…infidelity…and grace…yes, an absolute slathering of grace.

As I mentioned earlier in this book, the key concept that this world operates on is that you Reap what you Sow. However, when Yeshua operates with individuals throughout the New Testament and indeed for all of humanity, we see another concept which is grace. The phrase has become overused in today's society, and has seemingly been robbed of its power. However, the blood of Christ will always remain the way, the truth and life itself. And this sacrifice will always be the single, most critical act in humanity, shining a light on what Amazing Grace is. Reaping a positive harvest that you did not sow, or even deserve.

"But he was pierced for our transgressions, he was crushed for our iniquities; the punishment that brought us peace was on him, and by his wounds we are healed.

– Isaiah 53 verse 5

When I truly think about this…the idea of being treated in a way contrary to what the sins I have sown in my life deserve…I find it near on impossible not to be filled with gratitude.

But it doesn't stop there. Let's look some more at what Yeshua exclaims;

"My Father's house has many rooms; if that were not so, would I have told you that I am going there to prepare a place for you?"

– John 14 verse 2

How can I not take a step back and think, "wow, am I really deserving of that?!" Why is such abounding grace finding its way to my door; and what should my response be?

Answer? Gratitude!

Giving thanks with a grateful heart and an upright mind in all circumstances. Because YAH who loved me so intricately from the very first moment I was conceived (*see Psalm 139 verses 13 - 16*), has and is still doing so much for me. And it's only when I set aside time to stand in a place of gratitude, that I can remember my many blessings and count them one by one.

The story of the Samaritan woman teaches us about this grace. Not only was she an adulterous woman living in sin. She was also at the well, on her own, in the middle of the day. Culturally this may suggest she was ostracised from the other women in the community. Yet the Messiah found her, showed her grace, and her gratitude led her back to the community, bringing many more souls to the knowledge of the true saviour of the world.

Final Exhortation on Faithful

Although this chapter has been a smaller one, its importance cannot be overstated! The ability to set aside time amidst today's fast paced society, where time never seems to exist, is a rare but valuable skill. To show loyalty to The One who called us from the womb, by setting aside specific days for Him. Setting aside all your best laid plans. Operating in a mode of trust, sprinkled with intentional deeds. Living in a perpetual state of gratitude. Well, this is how you start to become a disciple of Yeshua; ready to take up your cross and follow Him.

It's important to recognise that these are not one-off acts that you do in the early journeys of your faith. They are persistent spiritual disciplines (get it?) that enhance your faith and allow the roots to go deep. It's these spiritual disciplines that continue to keep expanding your biblical understanding, so you are not swayed into the non-biblical traditions of men (e.g. Easter, Lent, Christmas), but rather remain rooted in the things YAH seeks from humanity.

These disciplines aid you in your reading of the Old and the New Testament. They can also be accompanied with reading of books from the apocrypha, that can bring some of the canonical stories to life. A great example of this is the Genesis 6 story, where some of the apocrypha books go deeper into the unnatural union and improper activities between spiritual beings and humans. These activities were a key reason why the flood happened during Noah's time. This knowledge also adds another layer of understanding behind Yeshua's comment, "As in the Days of Noah".

Your faith journey is the one part of your walk with Christ, that is solely down to you. You cannot rely on a weekly sermon, or a monthly prayer gathering, to get that type of food. You need to feed yourself and as Yeshua said to the Samaritan woman; you can only get that food from Him. The Word!

A soul that is truly connected and faithful to YAH, is a soul that is prepared, "in season and out of season" [8] to preach the word. Thus shining a light and inspiring other people to follow their actions; disciples, making disciples, making disciples, ad infinitum…

REAL
– not an imitation or artificial; to be genuine

"He wanted to see who Yeshua was, but because he was short he could not see over the crowd. So he ran ahead and climbed a sycamore-fig tree..."- **Luke 19 v 3 to 4**

The story of Zacchaeus is often told from the perspective of what happens after the tree; the dinner with Yeshua, alongside the acts of repentance. It sounds like one of those evenings some Christians dream of having at some point, bringing souls to Christ over some tasty food like fried chicken. However, there is something deeper in the first part of the story of Zacchaeus that often gets missed. It's a great way to identify how our approach to Yeshua, can trigger a chain **reaction of events, that lead to something beautiful…**

Throughout Luke chapter 19, we learn a few things about Zacchaeus along the journey;

- He's a chief tax collector, which means he'd probably defrauded people of their money
    - His exclamation to Yeshua about repaying 4x times what he'd cheated confirms this
- He was a short man, but he was good at climbing trees; sycamore ones to be precise
- He had lots of money, and was in a position to give half of his possessions to the poor
- He desperately wanted to see Yeshua in that moment

These insights show us that at the point Yeshua is approaching Zacchaeus, he isn't in what we may refer to as a "ready" state to meet his maker in the flesh. Yet there is something very real in his approach to Yeshua, that causes Him to pause. It's like when the woman touches the hem of His garment, or like when the rich young man causes Yeshua to stop and look at him with a deep love.

All these people have one key thing in common…they come to that moment just as they are! Real, Unfiltered, and Uninhibited!

When you come before YAH just as you are, something happens in the Spirit realm. It is an act of humility, recognising that you don't have what it takes to make you holy and righteous (right standing) before YAH. Rather, you put your faith in Yeshua to clothe you in that righteousness, to allow you to approach the throne of grace with confidence.

We're going to delve a little deeper into understanding who we are, to allow us to come as we are. However, before we start I need to make one thing clear…

There is a big difference between coming just as you are in humility and expectancy; versus coming just as you are with no care, reverence or regard for who it is you're coming before!

Want to understand what I mean more? Read the book of Leviticus and learn what it means to be Holy before YHWH! Yes, the blood of Yeshua makes us acceptable to enter the Holiest place, but make sure you approach that Throne with a recognition of who He is!

So, with that out the way, how do we begin to understand who we actually are?

NB; this section won't be talking about purpose. We'll touch on that later in the book...

How you got to where you are today

In the Old Testament, there are many laws that talk about tithing, finance and wealth...and all the things you are to do with them. However, there is no direct law linked to the concept of taxing, even though we know it existed. We see Nehemiah dealing with it in his time. We also see King Saul promising to make the person who defeats Goliath, exempt altogether from taxes in Israel.

As we move into the New Testament, the apostle Paul writing to the church in Rome (Chapter 13) suggests that a tax collector was no less doing their job before YAH, than a minister of the faith. And even Yeshua himself paid taxes; although he used a fish to do it.

This idea of taxing, often traced back to Ancient Egypt, was very much a part of the Israelite lifestyle. Under the Roman Empire, the tax collectors of Israel who served the empire, were known for charging extra to furnish their own pockets. Interestingly if you travel to parts of Africa today, you see a similar effect where government officials will take more from the everyday man, to boost their own personal income.

For the small time that Yeshua was undertaking his ministry, Zacchaeus would have been the chief tax collector in Jericho. Whilst Yeshua paid taxes, his opinion on these particular ones was clear;

> *"... What do you think, Simon?" he asked. "From whom do the kings of the earth collect duty and taxes—from their own children or from others?"*
>
> *"From others," Peter answered.*
>
> *"Then the children are exempt," Jesus said to him. "But so that we may not cause offense, go to the lake and throw out your line. Take the first fish you catch; open its mouth and you will find a four-drachma coin. Take it and give it to them for my tax and yours."* – Matthew 17 v 25 to 27

Zacchaeus was collecting taxes from his own people, on behalf of the Roman Empire, which would cause him to be perceived as a traitor to his own. Zacchaeus would have known this; he would also probably be aware that Yeshua and his disciples paid their taxes too.

For Zacchaeus to be the chief tax collector, his progression to the top would have been the same as how many of us operate today in the world of work. He would have made personal choices, similar to the long line of tax collectors before him. Choices to accept the hate, and enjoy the wealth that came with it. In spite of this, something in Zacchaeus was stirring…

The world hadn't significantly changed the day Yeshua walked by. It was operating the same as it always had. Yeshua was not someone who was known as a rebel opposing taxes. Zacchaeus wasn't poor and destitute physically, so on paper didn't come across as someone who *needed* to see Yeshua. Yet, something in his heart in that moment, meant he had to see him! This stirring was how Zacchaeus got to where he was at that point in time. He needed to see Yeshua by all means necessary on that day.

So, something in your life has brought you to where you are today. Or something has stirred within you to bring you to this place today. Now what? Well now it's time to analyse and move forward!!!

Maya Angelou said, "you can't really know where you are going until you know where you've been"; and that's why it is key to understand how you got to where you are today. And that's where analysis comes in; gathering insight on the good, the bad and the ugly within life's journey…

The Good

One of the easiest ways to identify the good parts of your life and its journey, is to understand what brings you joy and what brings you happiness. In my native Igbo language, the word "Imela" is often translated as "Thank you", but its meaning is also tied in with the concept of "well done / good job". Think of it as an all-encompassing way of saying "thank you for doing a good job". Sound familiar?

> *"Rejoice always...in everything give thanks: for this is the will of YAH in Yeshua Hamashiach concerning you."*

- 1 Thessalonians 5 v 16 to 18

That's right, Paul is exhorting us to give thanks and praise as often as we can. Well actually all the time if we read the text properly!

I'm sure many of you will say "in the hustle and bustle of life, I struggle to know what to be thankful for..."

Well let me take you back to Zacchaeus. Did he learn to climb trees from his Tax Collectors office? I doubt it... If you're struggling to see the woods for the trees to drive a thankful heart, then get outside amongst the woods and the trees!

Despite Yeshua's earthly father being a carpenter, many of His parables *seem to* revolve around gardening, farming, agriculture...things akin to His heavenly father. Examples of this appear in Mark Chapter 4, where we see the parable of the Sower, the Growing Seed, and the Mustard Seed.

Getting back in tune with how the Creator operates, allows our imagination to run wild. It helps us realign who we are and what we should give thanks for. This is further amplified later in Mark Chapter 4, where Yeshua is in a boat with His disciples when a storm hits hard. It's a reminder that our Saviour set us an example to find that place of peace, despite the hustle and bustle we find in modern day society.

Can you now say, "I am calm; I am ok", despite what's happening around you? If you can, then all is good and you have something to give thanks and praise for - Mark 4 v 35-41

The Bad

Going back to the theme of analysing and gaining insight on your life, is a discipline that permeates the scriptures. I often used to have conversations with people, trying to point out the strategic nature of our Creator YAH. Being an analyst who writes code, I always refer to YAH's laws like an algorithm. Pieces of code written and spoken into existence that won't change, no matter how much we think "society has moved on", or that "these things don't apply anymore" …because they do! Taking that into consideration, we should adopt a similar approach in our own lives.

John chapter 15 is part of a section in the bible (chapters 14 to 17) that I refer to as the, "special time". It's just after Judas agrees to betray Yeshua, and just before he returns with soldiers to arrest Yeshua. It feels like the penultimate point of no return (before the prayers of blood[9]), where the wheels have been set in motion and nothing will ever be the same again. So, Yeshua spends some special time with his disciples, talking to them in what I'd picture to be a calm, caring and nurturing voice.

In chapter 15, He once more goes back to nature and gives the disciples the view of His oneness with the Father. There is a symbolic act here that we should mirror in our daily walk with Yeshua. We should be understanding and gaining insight on the areas in our lives that are dead wood. The branches that need refining, or even burning, to ensure we can walk and live our best lives in the light of Yeshua.

It could be acts, people, frequent situations; anything that is guiding our journey and/or the actions along that journey. Because if that dead wood continues to display in your journey, it will likely lead to one place and one place only…

The Ugly

This one is a somewhat trickier concept to explain. How do you know when something is a learning curve preparing for the next stage of life's journey, versus a barrier or dead wood requiring a purge?

Answer; Through the power and discernment of the Holy Spirit!

Sorry…there's no quick win or easy answer to this, or indeed to anything on the journey of life with YAH. It takes work. However, if through the discerning power of the Holy Spirt you're pushing towards YAH, you will be on the right road.

Now we've cleared that up, let's continue…

Guilt is an ugly trait that can seep into our lives via many routes. As mentioned before, it could be there to drive us to repentance and prepare us for the next part of our journey. However, it can also come into our lives through dead wood that needs to be removed immediately.

Recognising the power of guilt over your life and the power you hold over other's lives through it, is huge. It can be the first step to grabbing hold of that freedom Yeshua promised us. And it's that very same Saviour who shows us a way to break the hold guilt has on us when not dealt with.

In Luke chapter 13 verses 14 to 17, Yeshua and the people around Him, are criticised because He heals a sick lady on the Sabbath. It is clear that this labour of guilt had been laid on the Israelites at the time, making them fearful to do good things on the Sabbath.

Now it would have been easy for Yeshua to just address the hypocritical synagogue leader and put him in his place. Yet, He does something extra to make everyone around be "delighted with all the wonderful things He was doing".

What did he do? He replayed the story from a different angle. He replayed the concept of the Sabbath from a different perspective, bringing to life the hold Satan had on this woman that could not wait a day longer to be released.

Like a good VAR decision in football, replaying the action from a different angle helps bring to life truth in a way we never imagined. The ability to replay things from a different perspective, may just be the key to breakthrough. The key to break the chains of guilt stopping you from being who you were meant to be… the real you!

We were never meant to be in shackles; we were meant to be free. We were even at times meant to challenge the status quo and be a little unorthodox in our approach…

"…*I will celebrate before the Lord. I will become even more undignified than this…*"

– 2 Samuel Chapter 6 verse 21 to 22

So, when ugliness rears its head in your life then it's time to, *"throw off everything that hinders and the sin that so easily entangles. And let us run with perseverance the race marked out for us."* [10]

There are other traits that bring an ugly reality to our lives, stopping them from flowing how we'd like them to. I've alluded to some already in this book. However, we must adapt, show resilience, and have the ability to respond to what is happening around us, just like Zacchaeus did. If that means purposefully breaking down barriers to do so, then so be it.

Be led by the Holy Spirit as He takes you on a journey of understanding into, where you are today, and where you need to go next.

Final Exhortation on Real

As aforementioned, if you're struggling to understand who you are or more notably where you are at today, then prayer and fasting will help you. Seeking YAH in this way through the power of the Holy Spirit, will give you discernment into that. However, it is also key to remember that no man is an island.

For all the occasions Yeshua went away to be alone for a period of time, He always returned to His fellowship. In much of his interactions with His disciples, Yeshua shared His thoughts on fellowship and accountability and how these play into reality. This happened even right up to His death, when He admonishes the disciples for falling asleep in the garden of Gethsemane; we are given an insight into what He spoke of in Matthew Chapter 11 when He said;

"Come to me, all you who are weary and burdened, and I will give you rest. Take my yoke upon you and learn from me, for I am gentle and humble in heart, and you will find rest for your souls. For my yoke is easy and my burden is light."

– Matthew Chapter 11 v 28-30

He was telling the truth, because the reality in this case was that His burden was easy. He just needed his friends to keep watch, pray, and be there for Him. This would help Him as He prepared for his weighty journey into the dark depths of sin. They say that a burden shared is a burden halved!

It's important to establish fellowships and it's important to establish them with the right people. People who have a shared belief system with you. People who can turn simple interactions into deeper communications. People who can help you convey or understand a deeper meaning to what you see before you; like Paul did as he talked the church in Corinth through the partaking of the bread and wine.

Zacchaeus probably didn't have *close* friends or people to *truly* fellowship with. Yet after spending time with Yeshua, he was able to understand exactly what was needed to turn his life around. An answer to the murmurings of his heart that had led him up the sycamore tree in the first place. Being real is about knowing who you are and showing up as you are.

As you seek to bring your real self to the table, beware of today's society that is littered with fake lifestyles and general falsehoods. On the surface statements such as, "live your best life" … "make great choices" … "be true to yourself", sound great. However, they are entangled in a web of lies, that basically seeks to establish a, *'do as thou will'* approach to living!

This is not YAH's will and having the right people around you from an accountability and guidance perspective, will help you see that.

A good mix of reality allows you to be who you are, but ready to be changed into who you're going to be;

- Faith, mixed with Deeds
- Feelings, mixed with analytical thinking
- Loving use of today's wealth, mixed with storing up treasures in heaven

I'll finish with Peter showing us an example of bringing a mix and blend of reality to the table. He brings a logical suggestion, during a wow moment. Raising his eyes to the sky, but keeping his feet on the ground…

The Transfiguration

After six days Jesus took Peter, James and John with him and led them up a high mountain, where they were all alone. There he was transfigured before them. His clothes became dazzling White, Whiter than anyone in the world could bleach them. And there appeared before them Elijah and Moses, who were talking with Jesus.

Peter said to Jesus, "Rabbi, it is good for us to be here. Let us put up three shelters—one for you, one for Moses and one for Elijah." (He did not know what to say, they were so frightened.) – Mark Chapter 9 v 2 to 6

INTEGRITY
– Being honest with strong morals, adhering to them even in the dark

"But you have neglected the more important matters of the law—justice, mercy and faithfulness"- **Matthew 23 v 23**

When it comes to walking the tight rope that is Integrity, we see many pitfalls waiting to snare us at every turn. Whenever you look at the fall of any great preacher, teacher, or government leader…it's usually down to a failure in the integrity department. What they did, did not line up with what they said, or what we'd expect them to do!
It's no coincidence that many governments, institutions and even churches are failing today, because the ability to maintain this act is lacking.

However, all is not lost...

The bible gives us some clear indications around integrity, highlighting both the pitfalls and the triumphs. It brings to light scenarios where there is an ideal way and a right way, which don't always align [Uzzah and the ark anybody?!].

In this chapter we'll spend time looking at the inputs and processes we must go through as individuals, to make sure our output is always to do the right thing, even when no one is watching!

Prevention is better than Cure

It's amazing when you reflect on your journey in life and all the different phrases you've interacted with along the way. Phrases that maybe didn't resonate with your younger self, but now in your more senior years make perfect sense. Prevention being better than trying to fix something after the effect, has always been one that resonates with me more in my wiser years.

Some might say I have a religious zeal which can sometimes be overzealous, when it comes to my "foresight" approach in trying to prevent a problem before it actually transpires. Inherently, that can remove the concept of living and enjoying the here and now. It's a fine balance that I often get wrong.

Our Saviour Yeshua teaches us an easier way of managing that balance. A way to manage what goes in, so that we can ensure what comes out from us is good and true.

When He is taken out to the wilderness to be tempted by Satan, Yeshua is carrying the full armour of YAH. Often when we think about fasting, we imagine a scenario of tiredness and weakness because food has not sustained us. However, in this situation we see quite clearly that Yeshua is wearing the full amour of YAH and is ready to fight with all the power of the Word that is in Him. Every attack and tempting arrow the devil throws His way, Yeshua rebuts it (and overcomes it) with truths from the Holy Scriptures.

There is so much to take from Yeshua's time in the wilderness. One of the things that really strikes me is how much Yeshua needed to know the Word, because of how much the devil also knew the Word. And that shouldn't be a surprise, given the devil was a heavenly being created by YHWH, for a more wholesome purpose than what we see him engaged in today!

Understanding the lesson from our Saviour in this encounter, we see that Yeshua was able to prevent a problem that would have required significant curing. He was able to do this because he'd previously invested time knowing the scriptures (as seen in Luke 2 v 46 – 48). He hadn't sat around using His foresight to plan for all manner of issues. Rather He'd used His time wisely to ensure what had entered His eyes and mind, were the powerful words from The Bible. Appropriately balancing the now, with the not yet.

As I have said many times in this book already and will no doubt mention again; we reap what we sow in this world. It is the key principle that the heavens and the earth are built upon. The actions you take will always reap a result relative to those actions; positive or negative; big or small; now or in the future; but a result nonetheless…

Fight or Flight

When it comes to integrity, it is worth noting that you can still reap a harvest of negative consequences. How you respond to them can determine what happens next.

The reality is we cannot always be prepared for everything that comes our way, no matter how upright our walk and no matter what smart actions we take in our daily lives. There are 8 billion people in this earth (at the time of writing), and it only takes 1 person to disrupt your flow and add confusion to your sowing and reaping. I believe this is why Yeshua tells us to;

"Do to others as you would have them do to you."

- Luke 6 v 31

A world of people operating with this simple principle, would facilitate a better outcome for each individual balancing their reaping and sowing. Unfortunately, we are seeing increasingly the opposite in today's society. The love of many, as prophesied in scripture, is beginning to grow cold. In its place is the love for one's self, amplified through the social media, reality TV and technology. This is why it has become easy to label people in society, forgetting the significance The Most High places on names and labels.

It's one thing to recognise differences, but another to label people with them. We see this articulated in the renaming of Abraham in Genesis chapter 17, verse 5. For YHWH, every name and label has a meaning. It brings identity, difference, and belonging. Abram was moving onto a new stage of his life. He was moving from being an exalted father (Abram), to becoming a father of many (Abraham).

YHWH loves difference; that's why he knits us together (DNA stranding) with such unique specificity, thus our names and labels become important to that identity. However we must understand that though we are different, we must come to the Father in a unified way…that is The Way; The Truth; The life that is Yeshua. Why is that important when talking about integrity? Because Yeshua embodied Integrity…

Throughout the Sermon on the Mount[11], Yeshua brings us to a place of understanding that states;

There is an Ideal way and a Right way, but unfortunately these do not always align. Especially not in Yeshua's "upside down" kingdom.

It would be ideal to punch that person who punched you first, but the right thing to do would be to look the other way! It would be easy to love those who love you and be friends with those who it's easy to befriend. But what about the difficult people in your life? What about the socially awkward and the vulnerable, who may be the ones we're told inherit the earth and the kingdom? Is this still ideal?

We can see that this "upside down" kingdom delivered on the mountain top by Yeshua, has elements of integrity at its very heart – even though it's not so easy to live out in today's world.

We started off discussing what happens when you're faced with a situation you didn't sow into, but it's now down to you to determine what next. A situation that may not be ideal, or of your own making and choice. Will you follow the heart of YAH, "to act justly…love mercy…walk humbly"? – Micah 6 v 8.

Will you draw that line in the sand, that no matter the societal pressure, you won't cross it? Will you fight for what's right no matter the cost? Or will you flee? Avoid the situation, ignore it, and allow the negative consequences to continue…

These are the choices and decisions we make in the *unprepared* moments. The fight or flight response that determines what we'll reap next. It's like the rich young man who came to Yeshua in Matthew chapter 19 verse 16 to understand salvation. He already walked in the ways and laws of YAH, including loving others as himself. Yet something was lacking which Yeshua pointed out to him. He was now at a decision point and had to determine whether he would fight for that perfection; or flee (walk away upset).*

Final Exhortation on Integrity

At the start of this chapter, I talked about how integrity has been the downfall of many famous people over the years. As history moves on, we see more and more people from our childhood, taken to court and dragged through the coals, for acts they have committed clearly displaying a lack of integrity.

That said, in recent years it has become more acceptable for people who lack any form of integrity, to find themselves in positions of power and influence. I mean up until a year ago, the UK prime minister seemed able to do anything that lacked integrity, with impunity!

It seems more normal to hear stories in the media that celebrate people with a lack of integrity, rather than celebrating those who have integrity and show compassion to others. **The polar opposite** to the approach of the Messiah, who spotlighted the poor widow who gave with a heart of integrity; compared to the rich people who gave with a heart of stone. [12]

One thing we do know is that when all is said and done, we will all be held to account for every action we have taken in our lives. Every word we have said. Every seed we have sown. And although you may never see the outcome of all those actions in this life, He does! But even in that truth, rest assured that the word about you and your name is spreading right now, right here, on this earth…

Listen to what is happening here in John Chapter 8 verses 12 to 59;

When Yeshua spoke again to the people, he said, "I am the light of the world. Whoever follows me will never walk in darkness, but will have the light of life."

The Pharisees challenged him, "Here you are, appearing as your own witness; your testimony is not valid."

Yeshua answered, "Even if I testify on my own behalf, my testimony is valid, for I know where I came from and where I am going. But you have no idea where I come from or where I am going. You judge by human standards; I pass judgment on no one. But if I do judge, my decisions are true, because I am not alone. I stand with the Father, who sent me. In your own Law it is written that the testimony of two witnesses is true. I am one who testifies for myself; my other witness is the Father, who sent me."

Then they asked him, "Where is your father?"

"You do not know me or my Father," Yeshua replied. "If you knew me, you would know my Father also."

But he continued, "You are from below; I am from above. You are of this world; I am not of this world. I told you that you would die in your sins; if you do not believe that I am he, you will indeed die in your sins."

"Who are you?" they asked.

"Just what I have been telling you from the beginning," Yeshua replied. "I have much to say in judgment of you. But he who sent me is trustworthy, and what I have heard from him I tell the world."

They did not understand that he was telling them about his Father. So Yeshua said, "When you have lifted up the Son of Man, then you will know that I am he and that I do nothing on my own but speak just what the Father has taught me. The one who sent me is with me; he has not left me alone, for I always do what pleases him." Even as he spoke, many believed in him.

To the Jews who had believed him, Yeshua said, "If you hold to my teaching, you are really my disciples. Then you will know the truth, and the truth will set you free."

They answered him, "We are Abraham's descendants and have never been slaves of anyone. How can you say that we shall be set free?"

Yeshua replied, "Very truly I tell you, everyone who sins is a slave to sin. Now a slave has no permanent place in the family, but a son belongs to it forever. So if the Son sets you free, you will be free indeed. I know that you are Abraham's descendants. Yet you are looking for a way to kill me, because you have no room for my word. I am telling you what I have seen in the Father's presence, and you are doing what you have heard from your father."

"Abraham is our father," they answered.

"If you were Abraham's children," said Yeshua, "then you would do what Abraham did. As it is, you are looking for a way to kill me, a man who has told you the truth that I heard from YAH. Abraham did not do such things. You are doing the works of your own father."

"We are not illegitimate children," they protested. "The only Father we have is YHWH himself."

Yeshua said to them, "If YHWH were your Father, you would love me, for I have come here from YAH. I have not come on my own; YAH sent me. Why is my language not clear to you? Because you are unable to hear what I say. You belong to your father, the devil, and you want to carry out your father's desires. He was a murderer from the beginning, not holding to the truth, for there is no truth in him. When he lies, he speaks his native language, for he is a liar and the father of lies. Yet because I tell the truth, you do not believe me! Can any of you prove me guilty of sin? If I am telling the truth, why don't you believe me? Whoever belongs to God hears what God says. The reason you do not hear is that you do not belong to YAH."

The Jews answered him, "Aren't we right in saying that you are a Samaritan and demon-possessed?"

"I am not possessed by a demon," said Yeshua, "but I honour my Father and you dishonour me. I am not seeking glory for myself; but there is one who seeks it, and he is the judge. Very truly I tell you, whoever obeys my word will never see death."

At this they exclaimed, "Now we know that you are demon-possessed! Abraham died and so did the prophets, yet you say that whoever obeys your word will never taste death. Are you greater than our father Abraham? He died, and so did the prophets. Who do you think you are?"

Yeshua replied, "If I glorify myself, my glory means nothing. My Father, whom you claim as your Elohim, is the one who glorifies me. Though you do not know him, I know him. If I said I did not, I would be a liar like you, but I do know him and obey his word. Your father Abraham rejoiced at the thought of seeing my day; he saw it and was glad."

"You are not yet fifty years old," they said to him, "and you have seen Abraham!"

"Very truly I tell you," Yeshua answered, "before Abraham was born, I Am!" At this, they picked up stones to stone him, but Yeshua hid himself, slipping away from the temple grounds.

I wanted to show you the whole chapter in full on stone tablets, because it can be difficult sometimes when you're reading a book, to take a sidebar to read a full length of scripture. However, I wanted you to see the full end of what I would describe as a heated dialogue between Yeshua and His opposers. The dialogue escalates the more He speaks, with an outcome so severe it nearly ends in a death by stoning before His time.

You'll notice there are some areas in this scripture highlighted in blue. That is because they give us the backdrop of why Yeshua needed to have this debate; why He needed to provide real clarity as to who He is. It was not just for those He was arguing with, but also for those who were listening, hearing, and discerning who He was and what His name and legacy would be.

The Gregorian year 2020 showed us that death can literally be just a moment away. In that knowledge, we should be striving to leave a legacy of worth and one full of integrity. We never know who is watching us or who is being influenced by what we say and what we do. Just like Nathaniel under the fig tree who was surprised to hear that Yeshua knew him and knew about his integrity. [13]

You will be remembered by those who follow on from you. Remembered for what you did, who you were connected to, and what you were associated with. Whilst you are still alive, if any of that needs to change, do it now before the cost is too great. Just like Saul (who became Paul) had to in Acts Chapter 9.

Interesting theory: *Whilst the story in Matthew ends with the rich young ruler walking away from the Messiah upset; some church traditions suggests that the man did indeed return, sell all his possessions, become a follower of Yeshua, and go on to write one of the gospels. One for further research…*

COMPASSION
– Concern for the sufferings or misfortunes of others

"YAH is gracious and compassionate, slow to anger and rich in love."- **Psalm 145 v 8**

As I write this, I have recently celebrated my 10th wedding anniversary! Every year we watch our wedding DVD and slide show, but the reality is I can remember the day like it was yesterday. I remember getting out of the car at the church, to see our friends dressed up; realising after a few moments that they were dressed up to celebrate me and my wife. I remember my mum getting lost and turning up late; sending my wife around the block in the wedding car multiple times before we could begin. I remember watching people dance in the aisles to old school favourite, Sweet Mother by Prince Nico Mbarga, whilst we signed the register. I remember changing outfits from traditional UK to traditional Nigerian, as the evening festivities kicked into gear. Many memories from one of the best days of my life.

One thing I also remember and still hear today from friends, is how much love they could feel in the room. Not just between me and my wife, but in the message from the pulpit...the prayers and worship...the already married couples sharing knowing and warm glances...

Many expressions that capture the emotive feeling, classed in society today as love. However, like every emotion, this essence of love is temporary. Something more is needed to facilitate a marriage that will take you into your greyer haired years.

Love as a Verb

So, what about love as a verb? What about the love that expresses itself in action and deed? This is where compassion interacts with love; and this is where we start to delve into a deeper love.

Let's look at what insight the Word of YAH gives us about love...

15 years ago, I started writing a blog for Roots, with the sole purpose of trying to understand biblical love and how that foundation builds a community.

The blurb I wrote at the time went as follows;

> "Go Into All The World And Preach The Good News To All Creation..." Mark 16 v 15
>
> *Don't you find it strange how the first thing that comes to your mind when you're reading this verse is... "Here we go again, some Bible Bashers trying to recruit for the church!!"*
>
> *Why is this the case? What has happened in the past 2000 years that has distorted something so basic, into something so complex??*
>
> *Is the verse not a simple message of Love!? One that could bring peace and happiness in a troubled world today; Love!?!*
>
> *A Kiss, A Hug, A Faith, A Family; the thought that someone cares about you, is interested in who you are and the things you do. Is prepared to make time and space for you; that sense of belonging that makes us feel whole... Isn't that the good news!??*
>
> *We would like to invite you to join the Roots Community; a community that wants to see what happens when people come together, with no agenda other than to explore what it is to truly love one another...*
>
> "And now these three remain: faith, hope and love. But the greatest of these is love." 1 Cor 13 v 13

When you read that blurb, it's clear that I was struggling to understand why the concept of love was so distorted and confused; especially here in the UK. I wondered why showing care and compassion, could generate distrust and suspicion.

However, as I delved deeper into the Word, it became clear that the concept of love itself had become distorted. That was why *acts* of love, were sometimes met with negativity. Love was a command given to us by the Father in the Old Testament, and echoed by the Son in the New Testament. We were commanded to love one another with what the bible describes as a, "perfect love".

I often call the apostle John the emotional apostle. He was the disciple responsible for the 4th Gospel in the Canon and he referred to himself as the one whom Yeshua loved. Much of his writing in the gospel centred on the aspects of love and how Yeshua was the physical representation of that love. However, it's always interesting comparing his gospel to his later writings; especially in the book of Revelations after the state had tried to execute him but failed.

In the first book of John, there is a passage that looks at love;

> "And so we know and rely on the love YAH has for us. YAH is love. Whoever lives in love lives in YAH, and YAH in them. This is how love is made complete among us so that we will have confidence on the day of judgment: In this world we are like Yeshua. There is no fear in love. But perfect love drives out fear, because fear has to do with punishment. The one who fears is not made perfect in love.
>
> We love because he first loved us. Whoever claims to love YAH yet hates a brother or sister is a liar. For whoever does not love their brother and sister, whom they have seen, cannot love YAH, whom they have not seen.
>
> And he has given us this command: Anyone who loves YAH must also love their brother and sister."
>
> – 1 John 4 verses 16 to 21

In this passage, we start to understand the *verb* aspects that underpin love…

- We love because we were loved…the act of acknowledging being loved
- You can't love the invisible and not the visible…physical acts of love
- To live in YHWH, is to live in love…loving is a daily act
- To live in love is to live like Yeshua did…He committed acts of love
- Perfect love drives out fear…it is the above acts that drive out this fear

All those elements require an <u>action</u> to truly bring love to life. And that is why we can conclude that YAH is love. Because it was through His love for us, that the act of creation happened in the first place; bringing us to life. The great king David attempts to describe the intricate act behind creating a human being *(special words highlighted blue)…*

For you created my inmost being; you knit me together in my mother's womb.

I praise you because I am fearfully and wonderfully made; your works are wonderful,

I know that full well.

My frame was not hidden from you when I was made in the secret place,

when I was woven together in the depths of the earth.

Your eyes saw my unformed body; all the days ordained for me were written in your book

before one of them came to be. – Psalm 139 verses 13 to 16

This passage brings to life the meticulous care and design that weaves through our creation. It highlights just how beautifully, fearfully, and wonderfully made we are. And it is with that same love, YHWH chose His son Yeshua to be our Saviour from the beginning of time.

Let's look at this act of love a bit deeper…

In the Bible, the book of Leviticus helps bring to life the Day of Atonement. A simple summary of Atonement is that…

1. YAH has and always will want to dwell with humanity;
2. Humanity sins;
3. YAH is too Holy to be associated with those sins;
4. A sacrifice (scapegoat) is required to make atonement for those sins;
5. The atonement requires blood, which is the soul of the being

The concept of the perfect sacrifice set apart from the beginning of time for our sin, is not just one that speaks of foreknowledge. It speaks more of a deep compassion and love. Fast forward several millennia to Mark chapter 15 and you see the culmination of that perfect sacrifice, in Yeshua on the cross.

I mean, why should the Father sacrifice his only Son for us?

The son He loves greatly and gives all His authority and power to...

Why should He seek atonement for us, to enable us to dwell in His presence?

Because that has been His desire from the beginning...

From walking in the garden with Adam, to wanting to meet the Israelites on Mount Sinai. From the beginning and up till now, YAH has always wanted to dwell with humanity. That is an act of love and that is why YAH is love!

Now what do you think about perfect love?

Does this sound like the definition I shared previously for compassion ... *"Concern for the misfortune of others"* and doing something about it?!

Does this not show us how love and compassion; faith and deeds; are as one!?!

If you're reading this and you're now starting to feel a swell within your chest, let me try and unpack some key areas for you to think about, as you aim to live a life of love and compassion.

Compassion Fatigue

At the start of this book, I talked about my upbringing. The complexities of operating in two worlds, whilst trying to understand and maintain my authentic identity. Growing up in the UK, I was fed an image of what need was. It was usually in the shape and form of someone who looked like me, surrounded by flies, with a belly the size of a car tyre. It was also usually accompanied with a voice over by what many now see as a White saviour.

As the Black Lives Matter movement grew in 2020, much was said about the impact White saviours had on the perception of what Black is. Charity organisations like Comic Relief made strong efforts to change the narrative and to change the image. However, as the world of 24-hour news, social media, and selfies has developed; the love of most seems to have grown cold.

Compassion fatigue is something that has been around (or at least recognised) for decades. For me growing up with perpetuated images of Black poverty, this is something I can completely attest to. The concept that you get so tired of another's struggles, you become indifferent to them, or worse angered towards them. Many of us suffer from it, but it is something we should make a conscious effort to challenge in our thoughts and feelings. Yeshua alludes to this diminishing love on the Mount of Olives in Matthew 24, where He is providing prophetic statements about the signs of the end times.

In the prophetic discourse, He speaks about a time when the love of many will grow cold. Yet, He prefaces this comment with something very challenging to us as individuals…

Because of the increase of wickedness, the love of most will grow cold

– Matthew 24 verses 12

Yes, the concept of becoming cold towards acts and feelings of love, is wicked!

Allowing compassion fatigue to become embedded in our soul, is wicked!

Increase in our lives of physical, spiritual, and mental wickedness, results in coldness towards others!

It seems like a harsh statement to say someone feeling compassion fatigue, has aspects of wickedness playing through their lives. However, we cannot ignore the truth of it and need to dig deep to understand why we're in that place.

Generally many people find the balance between their needs and the needs of others, a difficult one. Feeling like you haven't done enough or given enough to help those around you. Trying to be a cheerful giver but finding it more of a burden. Maybe that's why so many people use the phrase, "Charity starts at home!"

Let me let you into a little secret; did you know that the whole phrase from Thomas Fuller reads as below?

"**Charity begins at home, <u>but should not end there</u>**" – Thomas Fuller

Doesn't this sound like the command to love one another as yourself?

When asked about the law, Yeshua guides us to Love YAH and to Love one another. We unpacked this earlier in this chapter when we looked at the acts of love that YAH did for us. It's at this starting point we begin to find our way to loving others.

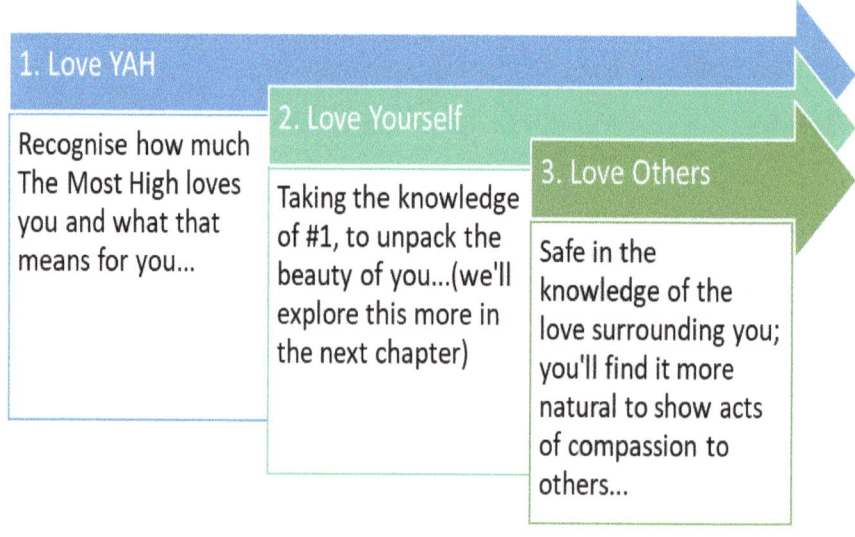

There will always be need around us; the Messiah told us that in Mark chapter 14. Therefore, we cannot afford to become fatigued with those needs. Acts of love and compassion are a command from YAH himself. If we start at home with ourselves, recognising how fearfully and wonderfully made we are, we'll find it easier to ensure that our charitable heart does not stop there.

Judgement

Something I've observed as more people gain access to social media, is a world that is quick to judge. Yeshua was clear on judging others, when he told the people on the mountain...

"Judge not, that you be not judged. For with the judgement you pronounce, you will be judged"

– Matthew 7 v 1-2

To be clear, this is not giving us a carte blanche to follow today's doctrine of "do as thou wilt", because you shouldn't be judged for "living your best life". Not at all; YHWH gives real clarity on what is good and what isn't. What is worthy of judgment and what isn't! The passage instead gives us an understanding of how our Saviour views judgement in this world, and the issues it causes.

Humanity has set a standard of what we deem to be good. What we deem to be desirable, worthy, and just. And anything that falls outside of that construct, is left like a leper in the corner. Therefore, the marginalised have become more marginalised, the lower-class population has grown, and poverty has not been eradicated from the world, despite an increase in the wealthy...Satan truly is the lord of this earth!

So how can we as individuals operate outside the way of the world? Well, no different to everything we've discussed in this book so far...

- It starts with YAH,
- Moves down to us,
- And then flows onto others

When we are faced with someone or something outside of our norm, we must follow the same approach to ensure we're don't stray into the judgement Yeshua admonishes us for. Every interaction should be weighed up before YHWH and His standards; yep, you guessed it, the Bible! From there we can establish what His opinion on someone or something is, and even take direction on how to approach the circumstance.

It could be dealing with someone that has a physical disease. Perhaps navigating the complexities of mental ailments and general healing. Even challenging someone on a particular lifestyle not in line with YHWH.

A song I've loved since I first heard it is, "Walk a Mile in My Shoes" by Cold Cut. The song challenges the listener to take a moment to pause before they criticise, accuse, or abuse. They're entreating the listener to put themselves in the shoes of another person; usually the person they're about to judge verbally. The bible makes it clear just how powerful that verbal judgement can be…

"The tongue has the power of life and death"

– Proverbs 18 v 21

The tongue is powerful and can be used for good and evil. Having compassion in how we speak and conduct ourselves towards others, is another key part of the acts this chapter has focused on. Use your tongue not to judge others, but to show compassion to those in need.

It's time to stop the blame culture and walk a mile in someone else's shoes. The blame culture we're surrounded by, is counter cultural to the life we're supposed to have. This is even more pertinent if we claim to have been redeemed by the blood of the lamb;

"Therefore, there is now no condemnation for those who are in Christ Jesus"

– Romans 8 v 1

Loss & Sadness

Another trigger for a lack of compassion and potentially one of the biggest, comes in the form of loss and sadness. When we as human beings feel abandoned by our Elohim because our greatest fears have been realised, or the worst has happened, we find it easy to become cold. Numb with the pain of searing loss that can only be soothed by the Holy Spirit, through a peace that surpasses all understanding.

After the turn of the millennium when Steve and I started Roots, we joined forces in prayer, with a couple who went on to start 'That Café Thing'. A small Chester based business, centred around coffee and the Gospel; (picture Costa meets the Disciples). The projects had a time of flourishing, but one of my main memories from that season was the personal journey of our two dear friends. Over the next decade, focus would shift quickly from social enterprises to the pain of childlessness.

The story isn't mine to tell and later I'll share the award-winning blog that Dave and Lizzie, along with others, have gone on to create to help people in this space. However, for me as a young millennial who had not experienced this type of pain before, I was gaining insight into what the song writer Stuart Townend meant by the phrase, "the pain of searing loss".

When you are faced with this level of sadness and/or pain, you go through a journey of emotions. These include anger, which let's be honest, is sometimes directed straight towards YAH Himself. However, there is something unique about the aspects of the Holy Spirit, which on reflection, let us know we should expect such pain to come.

Let me expand…In John chapter 14, the Holy Spirit is referred to by a few definitions; the helper, the advocate and/or the comforter (depending on the bible version). This essence of a caregiving Holy Spirit is also captured just before the creation of humanity.

The Spirit of Elohim was brooding over the surface of the waters

– Genesis chapter 1 verse 2

Some translations of the meaning behind the "brooding" used here, gives an image of the Holy Spirit encompassing the waters almost like the cradling of a child. There are many who talk about a concept, where an ancient civilisation (most likely angelic), existed before Adam and Eve. The idea is that the civilisation did not operate in line with YAH's will, causing a major destruction likely driven by the waters of the deep referenced in Genesis 1. This is the reason that the Holy Spirit is now brooding over these waters, because the earth had just been left in "waste and chaos". [14]

I won't spend time exploring how true or not the gap theory is, but the image of the Holy Spirit nonetheless is a powerful one. An image that existed before we were even created on this earth.

Acts chapter 2 is the conclusion to John chapter 14, where the helper/advocate/comforter comes on the day of Pentecost. When the Holy Spirit descends on the apostles, many things happen. Yet the thing I am drawn most significantly to, is the verse found towards the latter part of this passage.

They sold property and possessions to give to anyone who had need.

– Acts Chapter 2 verse 45

Is it a coincidence that after the Holy Spirit came upon the apostles at Pentecost, they had a heart towards compassion and giving to those in need?

When faced with pain, sadness, and loss, it is only through the power of the Holy Spirit that we can find our way back. It is through this power we can prevent our hearts from becoming cold to compassion.

Final Exhortation on Compassion

It probably feels like I've talked more about love than compassion in this chapter. However, the reality is that they are intertwined. Two branches from the same tree. Compassion is an outpouring of love; showing concern for others and doing something about it. It's not always easy to do, especially during a time of pain and loss. However, it is a command from YAH and one we should seek to live out in Spirit and in Truth.

I'm someone who likes to compartmentalise, especially if faced with disappointment. Like a child I put certain outcomes into certain categories and certain memory banks. Why do I do this? Because I believe it's biblical! The bible tells us in Ecclesiastes 3 that there is a time for everything. A time to weep and a time to laugh. A time to mourn and a time to rejoice. And this message flows throughout the bible, even into some of our more famous verses like the one you will have heard at many weddings…

"And now these three remain: faith, hope and love. But the greatest of these is love."

– 1 Corinthians 13 v 13

It's in times of crisis you hope for better … It's in times of trial your faith is tested … A time for everything!

From the beginning of time, it was clear that we will go through all the different aspects of human emotions in our lives. Recognising the season we're in personally, will make sure we're ready in and out of season to show compassion to others.

You may be in a season where it's time to rejoice. Great! Now may be the time to reach out to someone who may need joy in their life. You may be in a season of plenty. Great! Now may be the time to lend an ear to someone who is feeling lonely; someone who has maybe slipped off the radar recently.

You may be in a season of pain and sadness. There will be times of difficulty, which will make the concept of showing compassion a low priority. In those moments own your pain and share your experiences. You'd be amazed how many people are going through what you're going through, at the same time as you.

I spoke before about my friends who turned their pain into a beautiful ministry, by sharing their story to bless others. Saltwater and Honey (http://saltwaterandhoney.org/) is a ministry that embodies maintaining compassion for others, whilst dealing with your own pain. It's honest, brutal, yet faithful.

Telling your stories (aka your testimonies) often, is key to our faith. It speaks of YAH's goodness, even when we've struggled to recognise that goodness. It gives others permission to embrace whatever season they're in, so that they too can continue to love YAH, love themselves, and love others.

Yeshua told us that the love of many would grow cold in the latter days and that is where we are now. It's more important than ever to keep our oil lamps trim, but also continue to bless and show compassion to others. Compassion is like a muscle. The more you work it, the better it works! Let's get back to compassion today and enhance the society around us, especially for those on the edge of society like the vulnerable and homeless. It's what Yeshua did and taught through so many different messages, e.g.

- Creating places of safety,
- Being the positive change,
- Random acts of kindness,
- Working in the background to make someone else's life better,
- Increasing your capacity for forgiveness (77 x 7 times I believe?!)

This isn't a social gospel I'm trying to preach, but I am trying to bring forth the "doing" side of our faith; often lost because we believe we're "saved". Yet, faith without deeds is dead and those deeds are rooted in the Torah. Law's, statutes, and commandments that create a heavenly society here on earth. Compassion; the doing side of love that demands presence, not just presents!

AUTHENTICITY
– the quality of being real or true

"Salt is good, but if it loses its saltiness, how can it be made salty again?"- **Luke 14 v 34**

Do you reflect on how small you are in the big picture of the Heavens and the Earth? This infinite concept that is bound only by He who has no end and no beginning? It makes me feel small and somewhat insignificant. That's an extreme view! On the other hand, I do see many people who fall on the other side of the coin, carrying a significant self-importance, with no regard for what has preceded them or what will follow after them.

Coming from a heritage that is eastern in its approach, whilst growing up in a westernised society, has highlighted many differences to me. One of them is the way we treat elders. In the UK I see a lot of disrespect for those in the later years of their life. Until recently it was commonplace for a teenager to abuse an elderly person verbally and physically. When you get to a certain age, you find yourself on the outside of society, often sent to a care home to languish until your days end.

I know that again I'm being extreme here, but there is an obvious push in the western world to focus more attention onto our younger generations. Consistently seeking to lower the voting age, targeting younger and younger activists, exposing young people with little wisdom into positions of responsibility and impact…the list could go on. That in turn drives a lesser focus on the elderly, and by definition a society that over time has eroded and lost its substance.

Now whilst I'm not against young people being championed; I was a youth worker for a decade myself; I am drawn back to the source to get a better understanding of how society should look. There are occasions where young people come to the forefront with wisdom and might in the story of Israel; Samuel, David, and Josiah to name but a few. However, the usual manner of things is to give respect, honour, and attention to your elders. This is a practice that still happens very much in eastern influenced societies today. It has long been a mystery that many western societies cannot understand. Why do impoverished eastern communities, still contain such happiness and love, and seem less prone to loneliness and suicide?

The map below brings this to life, with the more impoverished areas having a generally lower suicide rate…

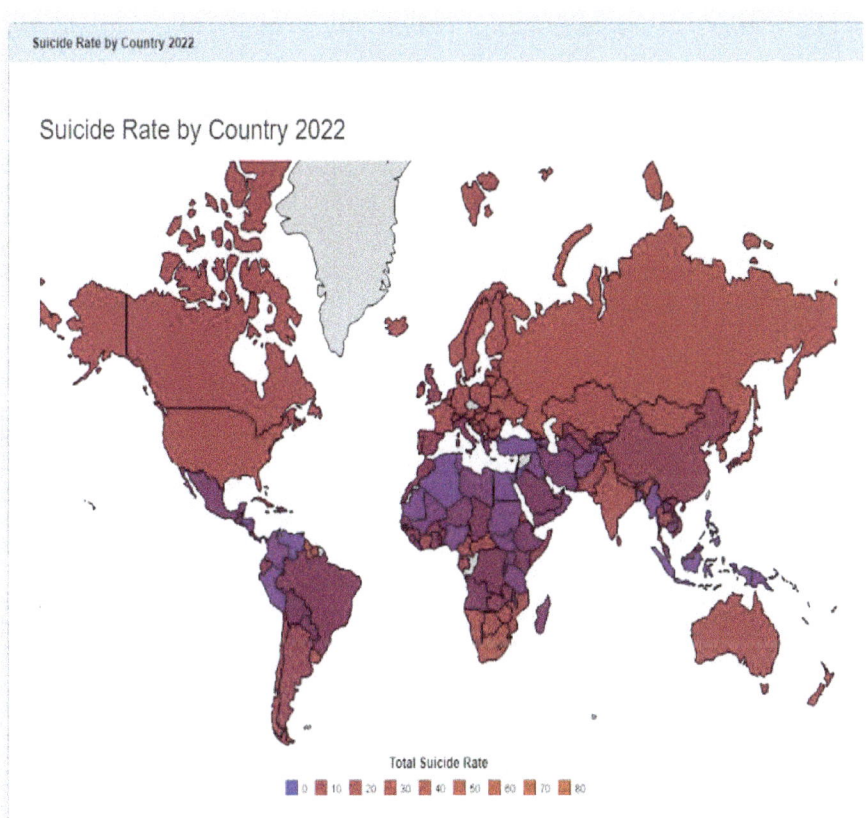

A map of suicide rates by country, sourced from https://worldpopulationreview.com/

Like the pearl of great price referred to in Matthew chapter 13 verse 46; when something is of worth, nothing material will ever match it. An example of that pearl would be happiness and love…

Having an appreciation of elders has allowed me to recognise where my story fits into the bigger picture. I was blessed to be fostered by an elderly couple, who took me in as a toddler when they were in their 50s/60s. That love and respect for them and from them as elders, gave me a healthy appreciation for all my family elders.

This appreciation helped me understand more about my wider family story, and my part in that story.
It taught me about my parents journey to the UK, and how they united despite differing backgrounds.

I learnt to appreciate what my Grandad did as a village herbal doctor. I recognised how that impacted the community around him, as well as my Dad and his brother.

So many insights that have an impact on who I am today. Many people from each generation with something of worth to bring to the table, helping me understand my role in life.
This understanding also helps my children and generations to come, understand their role in the story.

For me it is brought to life when I reflect on the writings in Hebrews, often attributed to the apostle Paul…

"And let us run with perseverance the race marked out for us"
– Hebrews 12 v 1

A clear concept that we have a race to run; one that is marked out specifically for us! Part of a bigger picture that precedes us and will follow on after us.

Authenticity, the quality of being real and true to who you are, must be understood with this same narrow and wider lens constantly intertwining between each other;

- Narrow lens; *Knowledge of who YHWH has made you to be…*
- Wider lens; *Knowledge of how your story fits into the bigger picture…*

Earlier on we talked about Zacchaeus, understanding the journey he'd gone on before meeting Yeshua. Well the reality is that authenticity becomes the main output of understanding that journey.

Going back to Maya Angelou's quote, *"If you don't know where you've come from, you don't know where you're going"*. This depth of understanding helps us break down the question so many believers and even non-believers have asked for centuries gone by – "What is my purpose?"

What is my purpose?

At the start of his ministry, Yeshua, his family and his disciples are attending a wedding. The passage was said to capture the first miracle Yeshua did in His ministry. The wine has run out at the wedding, which was not an ideal situation for an ancient wedding in Israel. Yeshua intervened and got the servants to fill up some ceremonial washing jars with water. They then took this to the master of the banquet and voila…a perfect batch of wine for the guests to enjoy later on in the festivities. [15]

I find verse 4 in this passage to be a striking one, because Yeshua's mum Mary has asked Him to intervene, to which he responds…

"…why do you involve me?" Yeshua replied. "My hour has not yet come."
– John Chapter 2 verse 4

What is Yeshua saying here? Well, I think there is a deeper sense of understanding to His purpose on earth. The gospel of Luke tells us that Yeshua begins his ministry at 30 years old, so it's fair to assume that at the point of this first miracle, Yeshua is in his 30s. Prior to that we get a glimpse from the Bible that He is interacting with Rabbis and teachers, reading scripture, growing in wisdom, finding favour on earth. This investment in growth, knowledge, wisdom and understanding, is what helps us determine our purpose here on earth.

The journey of life should not be a solo one, alluding back to recognising where we fit into the journey that preceded us and will follow after us. It requires learning and gaining feedback, whilst reflecting on how we interact with others in the good, bad and the ugly times. It also requires us to see what situations draw out the best in us, and which ones draw out the worst. A continuous learning journey that results in outputs you can be confident in, because you know they're authentic.

If you want to see this confidence displayed eloquently, read John chapter 5 verses 16 to 30, where Yeshua is responding to His favourite people – the Jewish leaders…

What are my unique gifts and talents?

When Christians think about gifts and/or talents, many are drawn to the parable of the talents. A summarised view is that we are given an investment by Yeshua and when He comes back, He expects a return on His investment. Similar to the concept of the Shrewd Manager and other business and reaping principles littered throughout the New Testament.

However I want to turn our attentions to a passage that is not regularly looked at in modern church ministry; and that is the sending out of the 70 in Luke Chapter 10 verses 1 to 23.

A sure-fire way to identify the gifts and talents YAH has given you, is simply to understand what things you're good at. Are you good at listening to others? Are you good at analysing information and then disseminating it? Are you musical? The list could go on…

However, there's something precious going on in this passage from Luke; it's what I call parental guidance. Yeshua gives the disciples that he sends out some guidelines, a framework to operate in, and a clear view of what good looks like. He then leaves them to it! Wow!

Assuming you read the gospels as a combined timeline, by the time you get to Luke chapter 10, you'll have learnt a lot about the 12 disciples and how diverse they are. Increase that to 70 people and you can imagine Yeshua is dealing with a multifaceted team, who are being sent ahead of him into every place He's about to go.

This passage is a great template for leadership, and although the scriptures don't detail this next bit, you can imagine the freedom the followers had and felt within Yeshua's framework. Their entrepreneurial spirits would have been flowing. The different methods for sharing the message would have been in full force. The impacts would have been varied, yet great.

We can deduce this by the way they all return full of joy, speaking about the impact of what had just happened. In that moment, under the parental guidance of Yeshua, they had found their gifts, sharpened their talents, and learnt what their purpose was.

Leaving a timeless mark

It is said that as you approach the end of your time here on earth, you're struck with a real appreciation of your mortality. If you're blessed enough to live out your latter days in peace, you tend to reflect on all the things you've done in your life. You'll likely think about the lasting memories you'll leave behind; alongside the material possessions you've gained in your lifetime.

Life is short! A phrase often overused, yet when taken in context with the several thousand years of humanity, completely makes sense. We have little time to make an impact on those around us, and even less to leave a long lasting mark to be remembered for the ages. And even then, we've seen over the last few years how a reputation can be completely redefined after someone is gone, if misdeeds or worse are uncovered.

There are many books out there that give advice on how to leave a lasting legacy. Many focus on the financial side, but others will give you tips and ideas on how to impact society. However, I want to focus on two aspects that come from The Word which are 'Appreciation for others' and 'Winning when you've lost'.

Appreciation for others

Over the last few years, I have spent a lot of time in the book of Revelations. The letters to the churches have been an interesting read, because I believe we are in that timeline now. The time where Yeshua is asking us as believers, and indeed our congregations, which body of believers are we!??

The letters read as quite firm rebukes in many ways, with an element of final warnings to the believers. What strikes me within these warnings, is that for every church (perhaps with the exception of Laodicea), there is a recognition of the good being done in some way, shape, or form. Whether it's a remnant few holding on to their faith, believers pushing through persecution, or whatever it is, Yeshua calls it out and acknowledges it.

It's almost like… "all these things need to change quickly, but well done for doing this".

This is something we can take on as people to help cement the impact we have on those around us. We should never shy away from calling out the truth and challenging lies. However, we should do it in a way that shows compassion but convicts appropriately. We should do it in a real and authentic way, that isn't layered with falsehoods and fake impressions. We should also have the ability to recognise worth and good, amidst the noise. Then we'll know when to say thank you and appreciate others, whatever the circumstance. Giving credit, where credit is due.

People who have the ability to do that, are the people we remember and the people who leave a lasting impression on us.

Winning when you've lost

What does it mean to win even when you've lost? Well, Yeshua's crucifixion is an obvious example, but let me share a more personal story.

For the last 7 years, I've been the chairman of our local Christian Football Club. We play in non-Christian environments, with an aim to uphold our faith on the frontline. As part of my role, I coordinated a charity football event which took place annually for 20 years. The event attracts 20+ predominantly non-Christian teams, and over the more recent years a church team from Liverpool had regularly entered the tournament. Unfortunately, they had never managed to get past the group stage, or indeed finish higher than bottom in the group stages. That was until 2017!

The church arrives with some young Mane's and Pele's, a bus full of cheering congregation members, and a desire to win! They were awesome! They stormed the group stages and before we knew it, they were in the final. It would be amazing to tell you that they went on to win the competition with a real story of rags to riches. However, the truth is they couldn't find the net despite putting lots of pressure on the opponents. It went to penalties which they lost, and the story ends there…although it doesn't.

For the next half hour, the Liverpool church team led a time of praise and worship. Yes, that's right, a time of praise and worship in the middle of the football pitches, amongst the predominantly non-Christian-based crowd – 100 to 200 people. Lots of people joined in; it was a glimpse of heaven, right here on earth.

This is celebrating like a winner even if you lose. This is being unorthodox when everyone else around you expects the opposite or expects conformity. King David did it when he brought the Ark back to Jerusalem in 2 Samuel chapter 6 verses 14 to 23. He was unorthodox and just wanted to celebrate YHWH, regardless of who was there and regardless of what people thought about him. Even his wife perceived him to be a loser in that moment, but he didn't care – he felt like a winner!

These are the people who live out their lives not only in an infectious way, but in a way that is authentic to them. It's people like this that leave a lasting impression on you when you think about them. I mean do you know who won the 2016 Triathlon World Series in Mexico? I bet you don't know right?? But I bet you remember the Brownlee brothers?!

Many of us remember the selfless act of Alistair Brownlee, who helped his brother Jonny Brownlee over the line. Jonny had started to struggle under the conditions near the end of the race. His brother came to the rescue, forsook his own race, and aided his brother for the next 700 metres to get him over the finish line. South African Henri Schoeman went on to win that race, but the lasting impression for most people remains with the Brownlee brothers. The ones who won, even though they'd lost!

Final Exhortation on Authenticity

The brilliance you note in the character of someone carrying themselves in an authentic way, is due to the confidence, understanding and wisdom that sits behind that person. It's not something that happened overnight but has usually built up over a long period of time. Often littered with mistakes, feedback, and lessons learnt.

You cannot be the best you, or as generation-z like to say, "stay true to yourself", living as an island. This whole operating model of your own self-worth and continuous selfishness, is not healthy. It's also not conducive to understanding your purpose, living out that purpose, and leaving a positive lasting mark on society. The key to this is remembering those who are your champions; those who are for you.

Westernised societies have lost much of this understanding, but it doesn't mean that has to be the case as we move forward.

When Yeshua was about to give up His last breath, His final words showed understanding of the journey that had gone, and the one that was to come. He speaks to Mary His mother and to John the loved disciple and says...

Dear woman, look, here is your son!" ... (John), "Look! here is your mother, protect and provide for her!"
– John chapter 19 verse 26 to 27

Parents, teachers, family elders, close friends; whoever it may be that is your champion and is for you, is the clearest mirror into understanding who you are and who you are not. It's no secret that some struggle with family and find it hard to use them as a barometer to understand their own authentic identity. However, an understanding of what has preceded you is essential for every person. That, coupled with a deep understanding of scripture and how YAH works, is a recipe for success and a path towards a confident, authentic, you.

CLOSING REMARKS

Humanity is about to move into a time where each person will return, "to your tents oh Israel"…
What do I mean by that? A great sifting is happening; nations are being shaken; more and more people are questioning the meaning of life and their place on earth.

Many are going back to their roots to answer these questions. As believers, our roots should be found through faith in YAH driving everything we do. It should be the reason we wake up; the reason we love our family and friends; the reason we work and play; the why in our journey giving meaning to our lives.

How we live out that faith and how we use it to inspire and impact others, is more important now than ever before.

We are in the last hour church! Yeshua's return is around the corner. I don't mean like many evangelists have been saying for centuries and decades. I mean we are actually seeing the birth pains and the Messiah is right at the door. When the 4th seal is opened in Revelations, the pale rider of death comes forth to take ¼ of the earth's population. That would be 2 billion people's lives today! He precedes Yeshua's return, so we should know that death could come to us at any time now, more than we've seen before. There is no pre-tribulation rapture; you will be here for the fire!

With all of that being said, can you be sure you've secured your salvation through fear and trembling?
Will you be the one who held fast to the testimony of Yeshua?
Will you be the one who kept YAH's Commandments and was not lawless?
Will you have faith strong enough to withstand the Beast kingdom onslaught and its Antichrist ruler?
Will you have enough trust not to succumb to the Mark of the Beast?

These are serious questions we as believers need to ask ourselves and our congregations. The book of Revelations lays out The Day of YAH. It is a day of wrath and destruction, before we see any glimmer of hope and happiness brought through Yeshua's literal millennial reign on earth.

As believers we need to WAKE UP and understand the times and seasons, before we are left outside the banquet without any oil. Or before we are robbed of our salvation like a thief in the night.

Let the Day of YAH not be the day the church cries, but the day the church rejoices…

Let it be the day we celebrate with the great multitude from every nation, tribe, people and tongue…

References

[1] 1 Samuel 3 v 7-11
[2] 1 Thessalonians 5 v 18
[3] Luke 8 v 26-56
[4] Numbers 11 v 16
[5] 2 Thessalonians 2 v 10-12
[6] John Chapter 14
[7] James 2 v 14-26
[8] 2 timothy 4 v 2
[9] Luke 22 v 44
[10] Hebrews 12 v 1
[11] Matthew Chapter 5
[12] Mark 12 v 41-44
[13] John 1 v 47-49
[14] Genesis 1 v 2
[15] John 2 v 1-11

There are a number of Bible translations available, to help bring to life the depth of the Hebrew language for a western ear. Throughout this book, I have used the following translations to help emphasise the point in hand;

- New International Version
- King James Version
- New King James Version
- English Standard Version
- New Living Translation
- Amplified Version
- Tree of Life Version